50 TIPS ON HOW TO COACH A KIDS SOCCER TEAM (D2D)

Chris King

Contents

Chapter One

INTRODUCTION

INTRODUCTION

Coaching young kids (ages 3–6) can feel a bit daunting at first — especially if you've never done it before.

The good news?

You don't need to be an expert.

At this age, football is not about tactics, positions, or winning games.

It's about giving children a fun, positive first experience with the ball.

If they enjoy it, they'll keep coming back.

If they keep coming back, they'll improve.

That's the goal.

This book gives you **50 simple, practical tips** you can use straight away.

No complicated coaching theory.

No jargon.

Just clear, easy ideas that actually work with young kids.

Inside, you'll learn how to:

- Keep sessions fun and engaging

- Manage short attention spans
- Build confidence in every child
- Run simple, effective training sessions

Remember:

You are not just teaching football

You are shaping a child's first experience of sport

Get that right, and everything else becomes easier.

Let's get started

Chris King

***

View my most popular kids coaching book and online course here:

PAPERBACK OR EBOOK:

Reviewed by 37 readers with a 4.5 star rating, this is my most popular book.

Start with this book:

COACHING KIDS SOCCER - AGES 5 TO 10 - Volumes 1,2,3:

ONLINE COACHING COURSE:

Taken by 479 students with a 4.5 star rating, this is my most popular course.

Start with this course:

HOW TO COACH KIDS SOCCER / FOOTBALL (BEGINNER COURSE)

A simple introduction to:

- Coaching young players
- Planning sessions
- Understanding the basics of grassroots football
- Ideal for parents and volunteers just starting out.

MORE BOOKS BY CHRIS KING

Chapter Two

TIP 1 – WHAT YOUR ROLE REALLY IS

TIP 1 – WHAT YOUR ROLE REALLY IS

At this age (3–6), you are not expected to be a professional coach.

You're there to:

- Keep the kids safe
- Help them enjoy football
- Give them a positive first experience

That's it.

The children don't care if you've coached before or not. They just want to run around, kick a ball, and have fun.

If they enjoy it, they'll come back next week.
If they come back, they improve.

Focus on fun first — everything else follows.

TIP 1 – WHAT YOUR ROLE REALLY IS

Chapter Three

TIP 2 – MAKE TRAINING FUN (THIS IS YOUR MAIN JOB)

Most kids at this age are trying football for the first time.

If it's not fun, they won't stay.

Simple ways to make it fun:

- Keep things moving (no standing around)
- Use games instead of drills where possible
- Celebrate everything (goals, effort, attempts)

If they're smiling, you're doing it right.

TIP 2 – MAKE TRAINING FUN (THIS IS YOUR MAIN JOB)

Chapter Four

TIP 3 – HOW TO ENCOURAGE KIDS (AND MAKE IT FUN)

TIP 3 – HOW TO ENCOURAGE KIDS (AND MAKE IT FUN)

Young kids respond to positivity.

Be:

- Energetic
- Encouraging
- A bit over the top

Use simple praise:

- "Great job!"

- "Well done!"
- "Keep going!"

Also use actions, not just words:

- High fives
- Thumbs up
- Clapping
- Big smiles

Kids love this.

It might feel unnatural at first — do it anyway.

The more positive you are, the more they enjoy it.

TIP 3 – USE ENERGY AND ENTHUSIASM

Chapter Five

TIP 4 – PRAISE EFFORT, NOT RESULTS

TIP 4 – PRAISE EFFORT, NOT RESULTS

Not all kids develop at the same speed.

Some will:

- Run faster
- Kick better
- Pick things up quicker

That's normal.

Your job is to:

- Encourage everyone
- Reward effort, not just success

Examples:

"Great try!"

"I love that effort!"

"Keep going!"

Confidence comes before ability at this age.

PRAISE EFFORT, NOT RESULTS

- ✓ Not all kids develop the same speed
- ✓ Encourage everyone
- ✓ Reward the effort

- "I love that effort!"
- "Keep going!"

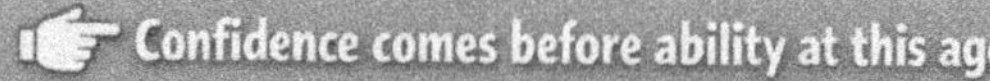

Chapter Six

TIP 5 – WHAT KIDS SHOULD BRING (AND WHERE IT GOES)

TIP 5 – WHAT KIDS SHOULD BRING (AND WHERE IT GOES)

Make sure parents know what kids need for each session.

Keep it simple:

- Drink bottle
- Shin pads
- Trainers or boots
- Jumper or raincoat

Also, show kids **where to put their things**.

Set up a small area using cones off to the side.

This is where:

- Drink bottles go
- Extra clothing goes

Tell them this at the start of every session.

Now when they need a drink or take something off, they all go to the same place.

No kids running off everywhere.

A simple setup like this saves time and keeps sessions organised.

Chapter Seven

TIP 6 – GET SOME BASIC COACHING EQUIPMENT

TIP 6 – GET SOME BASIC COACHING EQUIPMENT

You don't need much, but a few key items make sessions much easier.

If you can, spend a small amount at the start of the season. It saves time and makes everything run smoother.

Essential equipment:

- Cones (different colours)
- Bibs (2–4 colours)
- Mini goals (or pop-up goals)
- Whistle
- Small whiteboard

Why it helps:

Cones

Use different colours to set up multiple areas.

"Go to the red cones" is simple and clear.

Bibs

Helps kids quickly see teams.

Also great for simple games.

Goals

Small goals = more shooting, more fun.

Whistle

Useful for getting attention quickly.

Whiteboard

Helps you stay organised on match day or in sessions.

Simple tip

If cost is an issue:

- Ask the club
- Ask parents
- Look for a small sponsor

A small bit of equipment makes a big difference to your sessions.

HOW TO COACH KIDS SOCCER / FOOTBALL (BEGINNER COURSE)

Chapter Eight

TIP 7 – SIMPLE SESSION LAYOUT (USE THIS EVERY WEEK)

TIP 7 – SIMPLE SESSION LAYOUT (USE THIS EVERY WEEK)

TRAINING SESSION STRUCTURE (SIMPLE 5-PART PLAN)

I break my sessions into **5 equal parts**. If it's a 1-hour session, this works really well:

10 minutes per activity (5 parts = 50 minutes)

Leaves around 10 minutes spare for:

- Explaining drills
- Drink breaks

- Transition time between activities

This keeps the session flowing without feeling rushed or disorganised.

1. PICK A SESSION FOCUS

Before the session, choose **one main skill to focus on.**

For example:

- Dribbling
- Passing
- Shooting
- 1v1

In this example, the focus is:

Dribbling

Everything in the session should link back to this skill.

2. HOW THE 5 PARTS WORK

PARTS 1, 3 AND 5 – SMALL SIDED GAMES

These are simple games like:

- 3v3
- 4v4
- 5v5

Played in a **small area with goals at each end.**

Why this works:

- Lots of touches on the ball
- Lots of decisions
- Keeps kids active and engaged

Part 3 – Add a focus on the skill

This is where you **bring the session focus into a game.**

For example (dribbling session):

- Praise players when they dribble
- Give high fives for trying the skill
- Award double goals/points if a player dribbles before scoring

This encourages players to **actually use the skill in a realistic game situation**, not just in drills.

PARTS 2 AND 4 – FUN SOCCER GAMES

These are simple, fun games that help develop the session skill.

In this example:

Part 2 = "Gates" (dribbling through cones)

Part 4 = "Simon Says" (ball control + listening + movement)

Why these work:

- Kids enjoy them
- High repetition of the skill
- Low pressure, lots of success

These games help build confidence before going back into match-style play.

3. FULL SESSION EXAMPLE (DRIBBLING)

To summarise how it all fits together:

Part 1: Small sided game

→ Let them play straight away

Part 2: Fun game – Gates

→ Focus on dribbling through spaces

Part 3: Small sided game (with focus)

→ Reward dribbling (praise, high fives, double goals, etc.)

Part 4: Fun game – Simon Says

→ More touches, control and movement

Part 5: Small sided game

→ Let them play freely

4. IMPORTANT COACHING TIP

In the final part jsut let the kids just play

Try not to:

- Over-coach
- Stop the game too much

Instead:

- Encourage
- Praise effort
- Let them enjoy it

This is often the part they enjoy the most.

KEY TAKEAWAY

A simple structure like this keeps sessions organised, fun, and focused — while still giving kids plenty of time to play.

NOTE: WHEN TO ADAPT PART 1 (FOR NEW PLAYERS)

If your players are very new to football, you don't always have to start with a small sided game.

Instead, you can use **Part 1 as a simple ball mastery or basic skill block**.

This is especially useful if:

- It's their first season
- They struggle to control the ball
- They need confidence before playing games

WHAT TO DO INSTEAD

Use simple, individual or partner-based activities such as:

- Sole rolls
- Toe taps
- Happy feet
- Simple passing between pairs
- Basic dribbling around cones

Keep it:

- Simple
- Repetitive
- Positive

WHY THIS HELPS

Starting with basic ball work:

- Gets every child comfortable on the ball
- Builds confidence early in the session
- Reduces frustration during games

Prepares them for the small sided games later

HOW TO TRANSITION

After 5–10 minutes:

Move into your normal session structure (Parts 2–5)

Over time, as players improve:

You can go back to starting with a small sided game in Part 1

KEY TAKEAWAY

If players aren't ready for games yet, start with simple ball work first — then build into games.

Chapter Nine

TRAINING SET UP

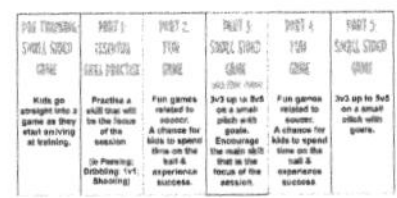

PRE TRAINING SMALL SIDED GAME	PART 1 ESSENTIAL SKILL PRACTICE	PART 2 FUN GAME	PART 3 SMALL SIDED GAME	PART 4 FUN GAME	PART 5 SMALL SIDED GAME
Kids go straight into a game as they start arriving at training.	Practise a skill that will be the focus of the session (ie Passing; Dribbling; 1v1; Shooting)	Fun games related to soccer. A chance for kids to spend time on the ball & experience success.	3v3 up to 5v5 on a small pitch with goals. Encourage the main skill that is the focus of the session.	Fun games related to soccer. A chance for kids to spend time on the ball & experience success.	3v3 up to 5v5 on a small pitch with goals.

Okay let's get started by explaining the first section...

PRE-TRAINING: SMALL SIDED GAME - Use this as children arrive at training up until the official training start time.

This is a great way to get the kids plenty of touches on the ball before the session has actually started! As kids turn up, simply get them straight into a game. There might be at least a 15 minute gap between the first child arriving and training actually starting, so why waste this time? Get them into a game and this helps them get extra touches on the ball and improve their soccer skills before training has even started.

As kids turn up, give them a bib and let them loose in a game! Parents can join in to make the numbers up to start with.

1. Have 1 or 2 small fields marked out (approx 20x15 metres). I know you may only have limited space if you are waiting for other teams to finish training but try and find a small area somewhere.

2. Organise the children into 2 teams as they turn up (have two sets of bibs on the ground ready to go). Try to keep it to a maximum of 4 or 5 a side so that all the players are getting plenty of touches. If there are more than 8-10 players, get another game going in the next square.

3. Simply throw a ball in the middle and away they go! Now they are having fun and getting better at soccer before training has even started! You can be talking to parents, setting up the rest of your session or joining in the game.

PART 1: ESSENTIAL SKILL PRACTISE - This is the time where we want the children to get lots of touches on the ball and work on their essential/fundamental skills.

Get them to grab a ball each and then show and tell them what skill they will be working on in this training session.

For example, if you have really young players, it may just be a case of showing them how to do Toe Taps or Sole Rolls (I'll explain these drills further on in the book). If this is the case, show and tell them how to do it and get them straight into it (they learn by doing, not by talking about it)! Then you can go around as they practise and help them out individually.

Stop them after a minute or two and re-show them. Get one of the kids to show everyone the skill as well - this helps build their confidence and if the other kids see one of their own doing it, they will believe they can do it as well!

If they are slightly older players, you may be working on Passing or Shooting. If this is the case, in the following Parts (Part 2 through to Part 5) try to make sure to emphasise and encourage Passing and Shooting.

PART 2: FUN GAME - A fun game related to soccer. This is a chance for kids to spend time on the ball, experience success and learn soccer skills through a fun game.

Use any drill from the end of this book or my previous three books on coaching kids (, and). Make sure to put emphasis on at least one main skill that you are working on in the session (ie Passing; Dribbling; Shooting; 1v1).

PART 3: SMALL SIDED GAME (with a focus on the main skill being practised) - Play 3v3 or up to 5v5 on a small pitch with goals (any more than 5v5, set up another pitch so the players get plenty of touches).

Once again, during the game make sure to encourage the main skills that are the focus of the session (ie Passing; Dribbling; Shooting; 1v1).

ADVICE: You can do this (encourage the main skills) by awarding double goals if the skill is performed in the lead up to the goal. **For example, if you are working on passing for this session, make it so that if a team makes 5 passes before scoring a goal, they get awarded 2 goals.**

PART 4: FUN GAME - The same as Part 1, this is another fun game related to soccer. This is another chance for kids to spend time playing soccer, improve their skills and experience success in a fun game.

Choose any game from the 8 at the end of this book, from my previous books, have a look online or my website also has free kids drills.

PART 5: SMALL SIDED GAME - Back to playing a game! 3v3 up to 5v5 on a small pitch with goals. Don't make any rule changes here. Simply encourage them to have fun and allow the kids to explore the game of soccer by playing against each other. Let them learn by doing!

TIP 8 - ARRIVE EARLY.

Arrive early so your training area and drills are set up. I know this isn't possible sometimes due to life circumstances, but if at all possible get there half an hour before. Then you are more relaxed, you have time to set up your drills, and can have a chat with the parents and kids. After all, soccer isn't just about kicking a ball. You want to enjoy it, socialise and have a laugh.

As mentioned in Part 1 of the Session Layout tip previously, when the children start arriving, organise them into a game straight away.

Enjoy the session! Forget about anything else that is happening in your life and just enjoy coaching the children.

TIP 9 - SET UP A MIRROR DRILL.

If you're not sure exactly how many children you will have for the session, it's best to set up what I call a 'mirror drill' (two of the same drill). This way, if you end up with more kids than you thought, you aren't rushing around trying to set up another area once training has started.

I like to set up the two areas side by side with a channel in the middle. This way I can see both areas and keep an eye on everything. Plus I can distribute balls to both areas.

Use one coloured cones for one pitch and a different set of coloured cones for the other. This is so it is clear to the children which pitch is which. (Then, for example, you can say to them "Team 1 and 2 on the pitch with yellow cones" and they know where to go straight away).

See the images below for how I set up my training area (this example has 12 children playing two 3v3 games and the coach in the middle).

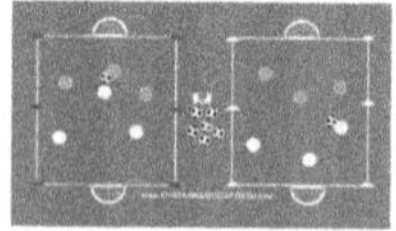

This is how I set up my games and position myself if I have two small areas. I can keep an eye on both games and distribute balls to both pitches.

TIP 10 - SAFE AREA (AND CORRECT SIZE AREA).

Have a look around the playing area before training and make sure that there are no obstacles or hazards that little kids may trip up on or run into. There may be gear from other peoples training sessions laying around so get that out of the way.

Also make sure that it is a good size area for their level of play. Don't make it so big that the kids will run out of puff after 10 minutes or are chasing balls for miles if they miss a pass or a shot on goal.

TIP 11 - HOW LONG TO TRAIN FOR.

Keep training to a maximum of an hour, once or twice a week. Any longer than this and children of this age will physically fatigue, plus they don't have the attention span for more than an hour of the one activity.

TIP 12 - PLENTY OF BREAKS.

You should give young children regular breaks for a few reasons.

Young children lose concentration easily, so every 15 minutes let them get a drink and switch their minds off soccer for a couple of minutes. Then they can refocus after the break and will perform better.

If it's too hot they dehydrate much quicker than adults so make sure to have regular water breaks if it's warm.

If it's a red hot day or an extremely cold one, you may be better off having a short, sharp session and finishing up early rather than trying to push through for the whole session. It's better to get 20 or 30 good minutes out of them than waste the last 30-40 minutes when they don't want to be there and aren't concentrating anyway.

Or if you can see that the kids have lost focus and aren't listening or doing what you need them to do, let them loose for 5 minutes! Just say "Right, you've got 5 minutes of free time to have fun." They can sit and have a drink, run around and do cartwheels or whatever they want. Then (fingers crossed), when they come back they will be ready to learn some more soccer.

TIP 13 - IF POSSIBLE, USE AN OLDER PLAYER TO HELP. Remember when you were in Grade 3? Who did you look up to? The Grade 4 and 5's! So if possible, try and get a slightly older player to help out with training sessions sometimes. Get them to demonstrate drills with you and get in amongst the children to help out.

Your kids will think that the older player is awesome! And the older kid will learn teaching skills and become a better person and player themselves.

TIP 14 - WHAT TO TEACH KIDS AT TRAINING: SOCCER SKILLS. Most children at this age will not have played soccer before or perhaps it's only their second season.

So you just want to introduce them to the basics of soccer which are: ***Dribbling; Passing; Shooting; 1v1.***

If you can focus on one or two of these main skills the kids will improve week by week.

Note: At this age focus on individual skills, not team tactics.

TIP 15 - WHAT TO TEACH KIDS AT TRAINING: SOCIAL SKILLS. Teaching the kids how to pass, dribble etc is important in soccer. But so is teaching them values such as working as a team, cooperating, taking turns and how to be a good winner and loser. If you do your job correctly, you will be setting them on a path of being a good person for the rest of their lives.

Side note: Make sure they are interacting socially with the other kids. Mix up the players when they partner up so they aren't always with their best friend.

TIP 16 - HELP YOUR PLAYERS BECOME GOOD ADULTS.

We want to develop good soccer players and win games of soccer.

But don't let this take priority over developing players with good character. We want them to become good adults. They may be representing their school or club for years to come, or they may drop out in a year and never play football again. It doesn't matter, try and help them develop into good adults.

As an adult you should know the difference between right and wrong, so try and pass some good habits onto the kids you coach.

Keep an eye out for non-soccer needs such as:

- Is a child shy? Give them a kind word and a bit of extra encouragement to help them get involved. They may just need some help initially and will blossom once they are comfortable.

- Does a player bully other kids? Maybe you need to have a quiet word and see if you can get them to help other kids and become a leader instead of bullying them.

- Do some players not help pack up or go and get balls etc? Try and make these things fun so they will feel like they're missing out and want to join in and help (make it a race or give out high fives to those that help).

TIP 17 - NO LAPS, LINES OR LECTURES AT TRAINING!

Repeat again: No laps, lines or lectures! Thou shalt not make your players do laps. Thou shalt not use drills that involve your players waiting in long lines. Thou shalt not lecture thy players.

Keep these three things in mind and it will go a long way to making sure the children enjoy training!

Why is this? The first two (no laps or lines) are because we want the maximum amount of time and touches on the soccer ball at a training session! If players are doing laps or waiting in line they aren't getting touches on the ball. They've come to soccer training to play soccer, so don't make them do laps of the ground or stand in lines waiting to have one kick of the ball every 2 minutes.

Imagine how many extra touches of a soccer ball children will have over a season if your drills *don't* involve waiting in lines or running laps without touching a ball?

"No lectures" refers to the coach spending too much time talking about what they will be doing that session and explaining drills. Children (and teenagers and adults!) usually only listen to the first few instructions and then they tune out anyway or can't remember all of them.

So don't waste time talking for five minutes when one minute would have been enough and the kids could've been playing for the other four minutes. They come to soccer training to play and run around - save the lectures for the classroom.

TIP 18 - HAVE A BALL AT THE CHILDREN'S FEET AS OFTEN AS POSSIBLE.

You may only have the children for an hour or two a week. So as soon as they are at training make sure to give them a ball to play with. If they turn up early, have a couple of balls out so they can have a dribble or a kick with you or their parents. As mentioned earlier, if there is room, have a small area and goals set up so if you get 3 or 4 kids early to training they can be playing a small game amongst themselves.

Imagine if they can have a ball at their feet and get an extra 50 touches on it per session than players that get there later? They will improve a lot quicker.

Note: On match day, if you have 2 or 3 extra players waiting to come on, feel free to give them a ball to kick around (as long as it's away from the sidelines). This will keep them occupied, they will make friends with the other players and they'll get lots more touches on the ball (probably more than the players on the pitch!).

TIP 19 - SHOW AND TELL.

When you're explaining a drill, make sure to ***show*** the children how it's done as well as explaining it. Everybody learns quicker if they are shown a physical skill rather than it just being verbally explained.

And don't forget to involve the kids where possible! If it's a passing drill get one or two of the kids up and involve them.

"Tell me and I will probably forget. Show me and I will remember. Involve me and I will understand."

TIP 20 - START WITH THE BASICS.

If it's their first season or two, start by teaching the kids the basics of soccer. Things such as how to trap the ball, how to make a simple pass, how to shoot. Get the basics right and they can build on this to learn more complex skills as they progress.

Here are a couple of tips on trapping a ball and passing a ball:

(From my "" book/eBook).

5 KEY POINTS WHEN CONTROLLING A SOCCER BALL

1. IMAGINE CATCHING AN EGG: When receiving a pass, players should cushion the ball with the instep of the foot to take the pace off. So imagine it as if they were catching an egg with their hands. They would take their hands down/back with the speed of the egg.

So they want to do the same with the instep of the foot when they trap/control the soccer ball. Don't be rigid and hard, **be relaxed and let the foot go back with the ball.**

2. MEET THE BALL IN FRONT OF THE BODY: Have the foot slightly out in front of the planted foot to make room to cushion the ball back in. And don't wait until the ball has hit the foot before starting to cushion it in - **start moving the foot back JUST**

BEFORE the ball hits the foot. Timing is key here, so don't expect the children to get it straight away (remember **Practice! Practice! Practice!** and before you know it, it will be second nature).

3. MAKE CONTACT WITH THE MIDDLE OF THE BALL: For the ball to stay in front of the body, control it on the middle of the ball so it doesn't bounce up or go under your foot.

4. KEEP YOUR EYE ON THE BALL: This is key so you can read the pace of the ball and focus on when to start bringing your foot back. It also helps in case the ball bobbles or moves just before it reaches you so you can adjust.

5. THE BALL SHOULD FINISH SLIGHTLY IN FRONT: When you finish the control of the ball, it should be slightly in front of you. This way you can make a pass without the ball being stuck under your body.

Also when controlling a ball, try not to stretch for the ball out in front or to the side of the body - move the whole body instead so the ball is in front which will make it easier to control. Quick feet! Be on your toes!

5 MAIN POINTS WHEN PASSING A SOCCER BALL

The main aspects of the passing a soccer ball are:

1. Aim with the non kicking foot

2. Open the hip up

3. Body (shoulders and head) over the ball

4. Lock the ankle

5. Hit the middle of the ball with the instep

1. Aim with the non-kicking foot

The ball should be slightly in front of the body, not stuck under the body. It should be at a slight angle to the body as well, not directly in front otherwise the heel of the foot will kick the ball and the other foot will get in the way.

So, for example, **if kicking the ball with the right foot, the ball should be slightly in front of the body at the 1 o'clock position**. Glance at the target and then look back at the ball (this helps with aiming but also to see if the other player is ready to receive the ball!).

Next, step to the ball (this can be a couple of short steps) and **plant the non-passing foot next to the ball**. Make sure to aim the non-passing foot at the target.

Key points to remember when stepping to the ball are:

- Bend the knee and point the toes of your non-passing foot towards the target.
- **Don't lean back!** The head should be over the chest.
- Don't stop completely before striking the ball - it should be fluid.

2. Open The Hip Up

The hip of the passing leg should open up as the leg is taken back. This allows the player to hit the ball with the instep of the foot with a nice open and flat contact which will send the ball straight. Try to make sure the foot is at a 90 degree angle to the planted foot.

3. Body over the ball

With the Push Pass, we want to do it along the ground so it is easy for our teammate to control. Therefore we **don't want to be leaning back** which may lead to getting under the ball. Also make sure players aren't reaching for the ball, as this won't generate enough power.

Players want to have their body (shoulders and head) over the ball. This will generate power and allow them to hit the ball in the middle of the ball and not lift it off the ground.

4. Lock the ankle

Older players most likely lock the ankle subconsciously when striking/passing a ball. But as a child learning the technique, they should be reminded to lock their ankle when they strike the ball.

To lock the ankle when doing a Push Pass, simply think of pulling the toes up and rotating them out slightly. This should create a solid ankle and they can strike the ball with good control (as the ankle won't move when hitting the ball and therefore not allowing the pass to go wayward) and good power.

5. Hit the middle of the ball

We want to be striking the ball in the centre/middle of the ball when doing a Push Pass. This will create a firm pass and the ball will travel on the ground. If the ball is struck under the middle of the ball it will lift the ball. If struck above the middle, it will go into the ground and not go very far.

So try to get the players to look at the middle of the ball as they are striking the ball and aim for that part of the ball.

TIP 21 - KEEP THE DRILLS SIMPLE.

I have listed some games/drills at the end of this book. What you will notice about all of these drills is the simplicity of them.

They are not over elaborate with lots of rules the kids have to remember. ***They are easy to set up, easy to run and most of them are lots of fun!***

5 and 6 year olds are just learning the game. So remember to keep the drills simple and fun and everyone (including the coach!) will enjoy the session.

Note: If possible, when practising a skill, try and pair similar levelled skilled players together. This is so players don't get discouraged if they can't do something that another player can.

TIP 22 - HOW TO GIVE KIDS INSTRUCTIONS FOR A DRILL.

Give essential instructions first. As mentioned earlier, you don't want to be giving long lectures to the children. So, when giving instructions on a drill, just give the essential instructions first.

This is what I do:

I explain the **2 or 3 main rules of a drill**, a quick demonstration and then say "Right let's go!" and start the drill. This should only take one or two minutes.

This way, it doesn't give the kids time to worry about what if this or what if that or ask ten questions.

Get them into the drill and then you can adjust as the drill goes along and answer any questions. After a minute you can pause the drill and just reaffirm what the main instructions were, answer any questions and tell them the next instruction (if there is one).

An example would be if you were running the drill "GATES". The aim of this game is for the kids to develop their dribbling skills by dribbling through as many gates (a pair of cones) in one minute as they can.

So I would instruct them to:

1. Grab a ball each.
2. Head to the marked out area.
3. When I say "Go!" see how many gates you can dribble through in one minute, trying to avoid other players.

This is all that is needed to start the drill.

Then after the first minute when they've finished, I would bring in other instructions. Such as "In this next round, can you use both feet and not go through the same gate until you've gone through a different one?".

Can you see how I start with the essential rules? And then once they have the hang of it and gone through it once, then I bring in other instructions. This helps by not overwhelming them and it builds up their skill and confidence bit by bit.

The final instructions of a drill that I may bring in is to ***"change it up"*** which is used to achieve a slightly different outcome. So if I want the children to learn to work with each other, I would now say "Stand next to a partner and now when I say 'Go' you will pass the ball through the gates to each other and see how many you can pass through in a minute."

TIP 23 - EXAGGERATE YOUR MOVEMENTS.

When you are demonstrating a drill to young children (or any age really), make sure to exaggerate your movements which will help to show the correct way to perform a skill.

Really over exaggerate and emphasise movements when demonstrating a skill.

For example, if you are demonstrating how to pass a ball, firstly step up to the ball and make sure to really plant your non-kicking foot next to the ball.

Then maybe step back and do it again but this time as soon as you plant your non-kicking leg, bring back your kicking leg from the hip so the children can see the movement clearly.

Then bring it forward with the foot turned out so they can see the instep is the part of the boot that will strike the ball.

And once you pass the ball, make sure to follow through with the leg in the direction you want the ball to go.

Once again, make sure to really over exaggerate and emphasise movements when demonstrating a skill.

TIP 24 - TEACH CHILDREN THESE 3 MAIN BASIC BALL MANIPULATION SKILLS.

The following three ball skills help very young players get used to the feel of the ball and get lots of touches on it. 15 minutes of this a day will see great improvement on their touch and how comfortable they are with the ball at their feet.

Note: These skills are explained in greater detail in one of my other kids coaching books **"Coaching Kids Soccer Volume 2"** as well as in my online coaching course where there is video and description of these 3 skills plus many others. Find the course at Udemy.com by copy and pasting this link into your browser or head to my website and click the link on the home screen:

https://www.udemy.com/course/howtocoachkidssoccer/?referralCode=CCFEDDB18FE0AAF8F1CC

3 BASIC SOCCER BALL SKILLS TO TEACH CHILDREN

TOE TAPS

How to do Toe Taps:

Chapter Ten

TIP 8 – ARRIVE EARLY

TIP 8 – ARRIVE EARLY

Arriving early makes a big difference.

If you can, get there **15–30 minutes before** the session.

This gives you time to:

- Set up your drills
- Organise your space
- Get everything ready

As kids arrive:

- Put them straight into a small game
- Get them active straight away
- No standing around

It also gives you time to:

- Chat with parents
- Set the tone
- Start the session calmly

When you're prepared and relaxed, the session runs much smoother.

Chapter Eleven

TIP 9 – SET UP A "MIRROR DRILL"

TIP 9 – SET UP A "MIRROR DRILL"

If you're unsure how many kids will turn up, set up **two of the same activity**.

This saves you:

- Rushing around
- Stopping the session
- Re-setting everything

How to set it up:

Create **two identical areas side by side**

Leave a small gap in the middle (so you can stand there)

Use **different coloured cones** for each area

Why this works:

You can easily manage bigger groups

You can see both areas at once

Kids know exactly where to go

Example:

"Team 1 on yellow cones, Team 2 on red cones"

Simple setup example:

2 small pitches

3v3 on each

Coach stands in the middle

Be prepared before the session — it keeps everything running smoothly.

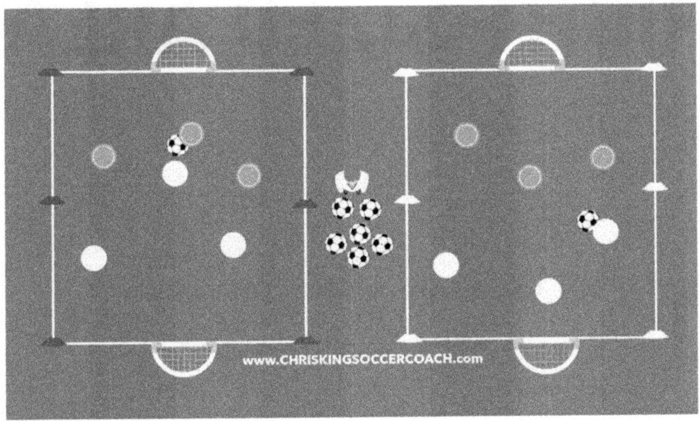

Chapter Twelve

TIP 10 – USE A SAFE, RIGHT-SIZED AREA

TIP 10 – USE A SAFE, RIGHT-SIZED AREA

Before training starts, quickly check your area.

Make sure there are:

- No hazards
- No loose equipment
- No obstacles kids can trip over
- Clear anything out of the way.

Get the size right

Don't make the area too big.

If it's too large:

- Kids get tired quickly

- Balls go everywhere
- Less control, less fun

Keep it:

Small

Controlled

Easy to manage

A safe, well-sized area keeps kids active and sessions running smoothly.

Chapter Thirteen

TIP 11 – KEEP SESSIONS SHORT

TIP 11 – KEEP SESSIONS SHORT

At this age, less is more.

Keep training to:

45–60 minutes

1–2 times per week

Any longer than this:

Kids get tired

They lose focus

The session drops off

Short, fun sessions are far more effective than long ones.

Chapter Fourteen

TIP 12 – USE REGULAR BREAKS

TIP 12 – USE REGULAR BREAKS

Young kids can't stay focused for long.

Give them a quick break every **10–15 minutes**.

- Water break
- Quick rest
- Reset

Why it helps:

- Improves concentration
- Prevents fatigue
- Keeps energy levels up

In hot or cold weather:

Take more breaks

Shorten the session if needed

30 good minutes is better than 60 poor ones.

If they lose focus:

Give them a quick reset.

"You've got 5 minutes — go have fun!"

Let them:

Run around

Have a drink

Reset mentally

Breaks keep kids fresh, focused, and ready to go again.

Chapter Fifteen

TIP 13 – USE OLDER PLAYERS TO HELP

TIP 13 – USE OLDER PLAYERS TO HELP

Remember when you were in Grade 3? Who did you look up to? The Grade 4 and 5's! So if possible, try and get a slightly older player to help out with training sessions sometimes. Get them to demonstrate drills with you and get in amongst the children to help out. Your kids will think that the older player is awesome! And the older kid will learn teaching skills and become a better person and player themselves.

Use them to:

- Demonstrate simple drills
- Join in games
- Help encourage younger players

Keep it simple — they don't need to "coach", just be involved.

Examples:

- Show how to dribble or stop the ball
- Join a game to keep it flowing
- Give high-fives and encouragement

It benefits everyone:

Younger kids stay engaged

Older players build confidence and leadership

Kids learn faster when they can copy someone they look up to

Chapter Sixteen

TIP 14 – FOCUS ON BASIC SOCCER SKILLS

TIP 14 – FOCUS ON BASIC SOCCER SKILLS

Most kids at this age are brand new to football. Keep things simple and focus on the core skills.

The main ones are:

- Dribbling
- Passing
- Shooting
- 1v1 (attacking and defending)

You don't need to cover everything in one session.

Focus on 1–2 skills each week.

Examples:

Week 1: Dribbling + Shooting

Week 2: Passing + 1v1

Keep repeating in different games

This helps kids build confidence and improve steadily.

At this age, avoid:

- Team tactics
- Formations
- Complex positioning

Focus on individual skills first — everything else comes later

Chapter Seventeen

TIP 15 – TEACH SOCIAL SKILLS

TIP 15 – TEACH SOCIAL SKILLS

Football isn't just about skills. At this age, it's also about helping kids learn how to behave and interact.

Focus on simple habits:

- Taking turns
- Sharing
- Working together
- Being a good winner and loser

These are just as important as dribbling or passing.

How to build this into sessions:

- Rotate partners regularly (don't let them stay with the same friend)
- Use small team games to encourage cooperation

- Praise positive behaviour, not just football actions

Examples:

"Great teamwork!"

"Nice sharing there!"

"Well done for letting them have a turn"

Keep an eye on quieter kids and help them feel included.

Good habits off the ball are just as important as skills on it

TIP 15 - TEACH SOCIAL SKILLS
Football isn't just about skills. At this age, it's also about helping kids learn how to behave and interact.
Focus on simple habits:
Taking turns
My turn after you!
Sharing
Nice pass!
Working together
Yeah! Nice teamwork!
Being a good winner and loser
Great game!
2 4
These are just as important as dribbling or passing.
How to build this into sessions:
Rotate partners regularly (don't let them stay with the same friend)
Use small team games to encourage cooperation
Praise positive behaviour, not just football actions
Good job!
Good habits off the ball are just as important as skills on it

Chapter Eighteen

TIP 16 – HELP PLAYERS BECOME GOOD ADULTS

TIP 16 – HELP PLAYERS BECOME GOOD ADULTS

It's easy to focus on football skills and winning. But your bigger job is helping kids develop good character.

Some will play for years. Some will stop next season. Either way, what they learn from you matters.

As the coach, set the standard.

Teach simple habits like:

- **Being kind**
- **Helping others**
- **Respecting teammates**

Look out for:

Shy players

- Give extra encouragement
- Help them feel included
- Keep it positive and simple

Negative behaviour (e.g. bullying)

- Address it early
- Have a quiet word
- Guide them towards helping others instead

Lack of effort (e.g. not helping)

- Make it fun to join in
- Turn tidy-up into a game
- Praise those who help

You don't need big speeches — just small actions, consistently.
You're not just coaching football — you're shaping behaviour

OTHER BOOKS BY CHRIS KING

Chapter Nineteen

TIP 17 – NO LAPS, LINES OR LECTURES

TIP 17 – NO LAPS, LINES OR LECTURES

Keep this simple:

No laps. No lines. No long talks.

If you follow this, your sessions will already be better.

Why it matters:

No laps

Kids came to play football, not run without a ball

Every minute should involve the ball where possible

No lines

Waiting = bored kids

Bored kids = behaviour problems

More touches = faster improvement

No lectures

Kids only remember a few simple instructions

Long explanations = lost attention

What to do instead:

Get everyone moving with a ball

Use small, simple setups

Explain quickly, then start

Coach while they're playing

Examples:

Instead of lines → set up multiple small areas

Instead of long talks → give 1–2 instructions, then go

Instead of laps → use dribbling games as warm-ups

Over a season, this means:

- More touches
- More learning
- More enjoyment

Let them play more, talk less

Chapter Twenty

TIP 18 – KEEP A BALL AT THEIR FEET

TIP 18 – KEEP A BALL AT THEIR FEET

You only get a short time with the kids each week.

Make every minute count.

As soon as they arrive, get a ball at their feet.

Do this:

- Put balls out before training starts
- Let early arrivals dribble or play freely
- Set up a small area for mini games
- More time on the ball = faster improvement.

Examples:

Kids arrive early → free dribbling or small game

Set up 2 small goals → let them play 2v2 or 3v3

Join in and keep it relaxed

Match day tip:

Substitutes waiting? Give them a ball nearby

Keeps them active and engaged

Over time, these extra touches add up.

More touches = more confidence and better players

Chapter Twenty-One

TIP 19 – SHOW, DON'T JUST TELL

TIP 19 – SHOW, DON'T JUST TELL

Kids learn faster when they can see it. Don't just explain drills — demonstrate them. Keep it quick and simple.

Do this:

- Show the movement or skill first
- Then give 1–2 key instructions
- Start the activity quickly

Even better: involve the kids

Use one or two players to help demonstrate

Let others watch, then try

Examples:

- Show how to stop the ball
- Demonstrate a simple pass

- Act out the game before starting

Avoid long explanations — they won't remember them. Show it, involve them, then let them play

Chapter Twenty-Two

TIP 20 - START WITH THE BASICS

TIP 20 - START WITH THE BASICS

If it's their first season or two, start by teaching the kids the basics of soccer. Things such as how to trap the ball, how to make a simple pass, how to shoot. Get the basics right and they can build on this to learn more complex skills as they progress. Here are a couple of tips on trapping a ball and passing a ball: (From my "Coaching Kids Soccer Volume 2" book/eBook).

5 KEY POINTS WHEN CONTROLLING A SOCCER BALL

1. IMAGINE CATCHING AN EGG: When receiving a pass, players should cushion the ball with the instep of the foot to take the pace off. So imagine it as if they were catching an egg with their hands. They would take their hands down/back with the speed of the egg. So they want to do the same with the instep of the foot when they trap/control the soccer ball. Don't be rigid and hard, be relaxed and let the foot go back with the ball.

2. MEET THE BALL IN FRONT OF THE BODY: Have the foot slightly out in front of the planted foot to make room to cushion the ball back in. And don't wait until the ball has hit the foot before starting to cushion it in - start moving the foot back JUST BEFORE the ball hits the foot. Timing is key here, so don't expect the children to get it straight away (remember Practice! Practice! Practice! and before you know it, it will be second nature).

3. MAKE CONTACT WITH THE MIDDLE OF THE BALL: For the ball to stay in front of the body, control it on the middle of the ball so it doesn't bounce up or go under your foot.

4. KEEP YOUR EYE ON THE BALL: This is key so you can read the pace of the ball and focus on when to start bringing your foot back. It also helps in case the ball bobbles or moves just before it reaches you so you can adjust.

5. THE BALL SHOULD FINISH SLIGHTLY IN FRONT: When you finish the control of the ball, it should be slightly in front of you. This way you can make a pass without the ball being stuck under your body. Also when controlling a ball, try not to stretch for the ball out in front or to the side of the body - move the whole body instead so the ball is in front which will make it easier to control. Quick feet! Be on your toes!

5 MAIN POINTS WHEN PASSING A SOCCER BALL

The main aspects of the passing a soccer ball are:

1. Aim with the non kicking foot
2. Open the hip up
3. Body (shoulders and head) over the ball
4. Lock the ankle
5. Hit the middle of the ball with the instep

1. Aim with the non-kicking foot

The ball should be slightly in front of the body, not stuck under the body. It should be at a slight angle to the body as well, not directly in front otherwise the heel of the foot will kick the ball and the other foot will get in the way. So, for example, if kicking the ball with the right foot, the ball should be slightly in front of the body at the 1 o'clock position. Glance at the target and then look back at the ball (this helps with aiming but also to see if the other player is ready to receive the ball!). Next, step to the ball (this can be a couple of short steps) and plant the non-passing foot next to the ball. Make sure to aim the non-passing foot at the target. Key points to remember when stepping to the ball are:

- Bend the knee and point the toes of your non-passing foot towards the target.
- Don't lean back! The head should be over the chest.
- Don't stop completely before striking the ball - it should be fluid.

2. Open The Hip Up The hip of the passing leg should open up as the leg is taken back. This allows the player to hit the ball with the instep of the foot with a nice open and flat contact which will send the ball straight. Try to make sure the foot is at a 90 degree angle to the planted foot.

3. Body over the ball With the Push Pass, we want to do it along the ground so it is easy for our teammate to control. Therefore we don't want to be leaning back which may lead to getting under the ball. Also make sure players aren't reaching for the ball, as this won't generate enough power. Players want to have their body (shoulders and head) over the ball. This will generate power and allow them to hit the ball in the middle of the ball and not lift it off the ground.

4. Lock the ankle Older players most likely lock the ankle subconsciously when striking/passing a ball. But as a child learning the technique, they should be reminded to lock their ankle when they

strike the ball. To lock the ankle when doing a Push Pass, simply think of pulling the toes up and rotating them out slightly. This should create a solid ankle and they can strike the ball with good control (as the ankle won't move when hitting the ball and therefore not allowing the pass to go wayward) and good power.

5. Hit the middle of the ball We want to be striking the ball in the centre/middle of the ball when doing a Push Pass. This will create a firm pass and the ball will travel on the ground. If the ball is struck under the middle of the ball it will lift the ball. If struck above the middle, it will go into the ground and not go very far. So try to get the players to look at the middle of the ball as they are striking the ball and aim for that part of the ball.

Chapter Twenty-Three

TIP 21 – KEEP DRILLS SIMPLE

TIP 21 – KEEP DRILLS SIMPLE

The best drills for this age are simple ones.

Easy to set up.

Easy to explain.

Easy to run.

If a drill has too many rules, kids will switch off. Keep it basic and fun.

What to aim for:

- Everyone involved
- Minimal waiting
- Clear objective

Examples:

- Dribble in a small area

- Simple passing between partners
- Small-sided games (2v2, 3v3)

If you need to explain too much, simplify it.

MATCH PLAYERS BY LEVEL (WHEN POSSIBLE)

Try to pair players of similar ability.

This helps:

- Build confidence
- Keep games competitive
- Avoid frustration

Examples:

Stronger players together

Beginners together

Adjust groups during the session if needed

Keep it flexible — it doesn't need to be perfect.

Simple drills = better engagement and more learning

Chapter Twenty-Four

TIP 22 - HOW TO GIVE KIDS INSTRUCTIONS FOR A DRILL

TIP 22 - HOW TO GIVE KIDS INSTRUCTIONS FOR A DRILL

Give essential instructions first.

As mentioned earlier, you don't want to be giving long lectures to the children. So, when giving instructions on a drill, just give the essential instructions first.

This is what I do:

I explain the 2 or 3 main rules of a drill, a quick demonstration and then say "Right let's go!" and start the drill. This should only take one or two minutes. This way, it doesn't give the kids time to worry about what if this or what if that or ask ten questions. Get them into the drill and then you can adjust as the drill goes along and answer any questions.

After a minute you can pause the drill and just reaffirm what the main instructions were, answer any questions and tell them the next instruction (if there is one).

An example would be if you were running the drill "GATES". The aim of this game is for the kids to develop their dribbling skills by dribbling through as many gates (a pair of cones) in one minute as they can.

So I would instruct them to:

1. Grab a ball each.

2. Head to the marked out area.

3. When I say "Go!" see how many gates you can dribble through in one minute, trying to avoid other players.

This is all that is needed to start the drill. Then after the first minute when they've finished, I would bring in other instructions. Such as "In this next round, can you use both feet and not go through the same gate until you've gone through a different one?".

Can you see how I start with the essential rules? And then once they have the hang of it and gone through it once, then I bring in other instructions. This helps by not overwhelming them and it builds up their skill and confidence bit by bit.

The final instructions of a drill that I may bring in is to "change it up" which is used to achieve a slightly different outcome. So if I want the children to learn to work with each other, I would now say "Stand next to a partner and now when I say 'Go' you will pass the ball through the gates to each other and see how many you can pass through in a minute."

Chapter Twenty-Five

TIP 23 – EXAGGERATE YOUR MOVEMENTS

TIP 23 – EXAGGERATE YOUR MOVEMENTS

When you demonstrate a skill, make your movements big and obvious.

Young kids learn by watching. If your actions are small or quick, they'll miss key parts. So slow it down and exaggerate everything.

WHAT TO DO

- Make movements bigger than normal
- Slow the action down
- Repeat it more than once

- Highlight one key part at a time

EXAMPLE – PASSING

Break it into simple, clear steps:

- Step in and clearly plant the non-kicking foot
- Pause so they can see it
- Bring the kicking leg back slowly
- Turn the foot to show the instep
- Strike the ball and follow through
- Show it once, then repeat it again.

KEEP IT SIMPLE

Don't try to show everything at once.

Focus on one or two key points:

"Foot next to the ball"

"Use the inside of your foot"

Then let them try.

WHY IT WORKS

- Kids copy what they see
- Clear visuals = faster understanding
- Less talking, more doing

Show it clearly, make it obvious, then let them copy

Chapter Twenty-Six

TIP 24 - TEACH CHILDREN THESE 3 MAIN BASIC BALL MANIPULATION SKILLS

TIP 24 - TEACH CHILDREN THESE 3 MAIN BASIC BALL MANIPULATION SKILLS

The following three ball skills help very young players get used to the feel of the ball and get lots of touches on it. 15 minutes of this a day will see great improvement on their touch and how comfortable they are with the ball at their feet.

Note: These skills are explained in greater detail in one of my other kids coaching books "Coaching Kids Soccer Volume 2" as well as in my online coaching course where there is video and description of these 3 skills plus many others.

Find the course at Udemy.com by copy and pasting this link into your browser or head to my website www.chrisking.com and click the link on the home screen: https://www.udemy.com/course/howtocoachkidssoccer/?referral Code=CCFEDDB18FE0AAF8F1CC

3 BASIC SOCCER BALL SKILLS TO TEACH CHILDREN

TOE TAPS

How to do Toe Taps:

- The player should stand with the ball directly in front of them.
- Now they put the sole of one foot on top of the ball while keeping the other one planted on the ground.
- Then switch feet so the opposite sole of the foot is on the ball and the other foot is on the ground. Repeat this.
- Players should go as slowly as they need to start with.

Eventually they will be doing it in a fluid motion. Build up so that eventually when players are used to it, they will be "bouncing" (moving one foot as soon as the other touches the top of the ball).

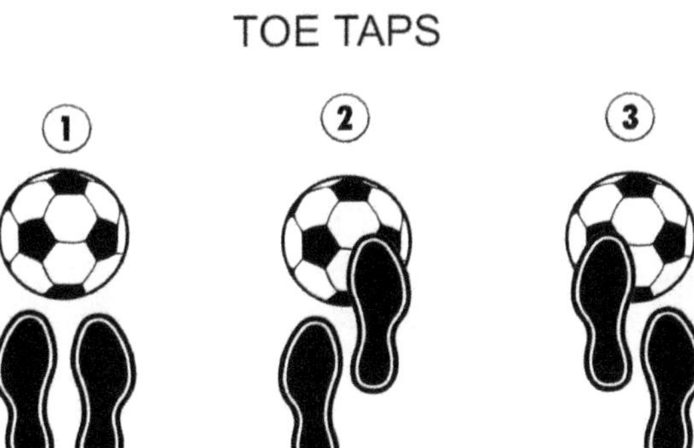

SOLE ROLLS

How to do Sole Rolls:

Simply roll the ball softly with the sole of the foot in any direction. Then, with the same foot, roll it back to the starting position. For example, roll it out to the right with the sole of the right foot, then roll it back to the starting position with the sole of the right foot.

Start by doing it in the one spot and then progress to moving around the ground doing it. Once they have the hang of it, players can roll it forward, backwards or whichever direction they want with the sole of either foot. They can make a triangular shape or square in front of them by rolling the ball with the soles.

And once they are comfortable, get them to alternate feet - so it might be to roll it out to the right with your right foot, then roll it out to the left with the left foot.

Advice: Tell the kids to do it at home with a ball while sitting on the couch, walking around the house or walking home from school! (Maybe buy a soft soccer ball in case they get carried away at home).

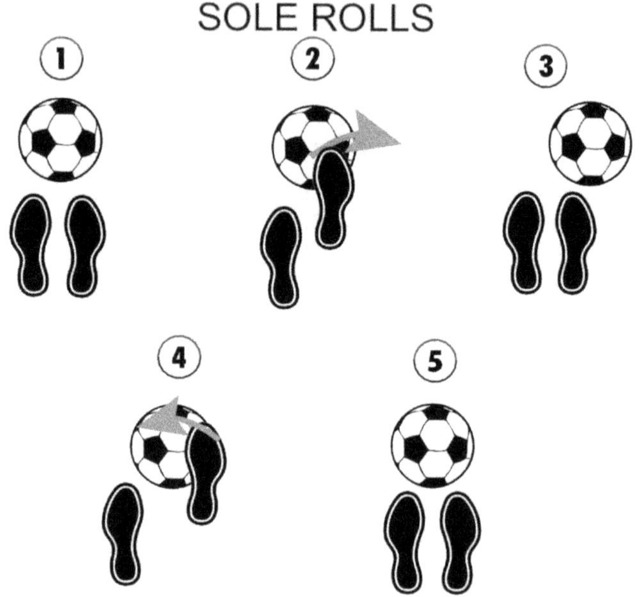

HAPPY FEET

How To Do Happy Feet:

Start slow jogging on the spot. Step up to the ball and have it between the feet. While still slowly jogging on the spot, lightly tap the ball with the inside of your feet so the ball goes from the left foot to the right foot and back again, continuously.

Advice: Keep the head over the ball, be light on the feet and as always, start slowly until the player gets used to it. Initially the players may not even be jogging, they can just stand there and tap it between their feet.

HAPPY FEET

use the inner part of both feet to tap the ball back and forth

Think of it like the old computer game Pong. This skill really helps with touch and coordination

Chapter Twenty-Seven

TIP 25 – FOCUS ON THE 4 MAIN SKILLS

TIP 25 – FOCUS ON THE 4 MAIN SKILLS

At this age, keep the focus on the core parts of the game. The 4 key skills are:

- Passing
- Dribbling
- 1v1 (attacking and defending)
- Shooting

Most activities you run should include at least one of these.

WHY THESE MATTER

These four skills make up the majority of the game. If players improve in these areas, they will naturally become better overall players.

You don't need to teach everything at once. Build strong foundations first.

HOW TO USE THEM IN TRAINING

Keep sessions simple and focused.

Examples:

Dribbling game → improves control and confidence

1v1 game → improves attacking and defending

Passing activity → improves teamwork and awareness

Shooting game → improves finishing and enjoyment

Most small-sided games will combine multiple skills.

WHAT NOT TO PRIORITISE (YET)

At this age, don't worry about:

- Complex skills
- Positioning
- Advanced techniques

Things like:

- Headers
- Volleys
- Tricks and flicks

These will come later.

EXTRA NOTE

Tackling is important, but it is usually covered within 1v1 games.

So you don't need to teach it separately at this stage.

Build strong basics first — everything else comes later

Chapter Twenty-Eight

TIP 26 - INVOLVE THE PARENTS

TIP 26 - INVOLVE THE PARENTS

You will find that most parents will enjoy being involved a bit at training. They are usually watching the whole session anyway. Simple things parents can help with is gathering balls, tying boot laces, picking up cones, etc. This keeps you free to focus on the childrens football development.

But one of the main things that involving the parents helps with, is they can see what their children are practising and what the coach is showing and teaching them. Therefore, when their child practises at home, they can help and show them the correct technique.

I also like to involve the parents in the odd drill if possible. One that the kids love is called Zombies. It's from my book "Coaching Kids Soccer Volume 2" which is available either by itself or as part of the book bundle "Coaching Kids Soccer Volumes 1,2,3" (which is a bit cheaper than buying all 3 separately).

Here it is if you want to use it at training:

"ZOMBIES"

This is a fun drill that gives the players a chance to work on their dribbling skills and turns. And it gives the parents/coaches a chance to act like a zombie!

1. Set up a square field (30x30 yards).

2. Ask any parents/coaches standing around to join in. They will be the "obstacles" for the children to avoid and will be walking around the square with their arms outstretched like a zombie. Get them to say zombie things like "Braiiinsss" "Graaaghhh" "Childreeenn" "Bananaaaa" and other stupid things or just general grunting noises.

3. Each player has a ball and must dribble around the square avoiding the zombies.

4. If a player gets too close, zombies should lightly kick their ball so they will learn to keep closer control. Or slightly push/bump the player to test their control and balance under pressure.

5. Make sure players are looking around as they dribble and practice turns and changes of direction.

WHAT TO FOCUS ON:

- Players keep close ball control so zombies can't get the ball.
- Use changes of direction to avoid the zombies.
- Keep their heads up when they can to avoid other players and zombies.

CHANGE IT:

#1. Make the area bigger or smaller depending on skill level/number of players plus the number of zombies.

#2. Make the zombies walk faster or slower depending on the level of players.

#3. If a player gets touched by a zombie they have to do 5 toe-taps and then they can continue dribbling.

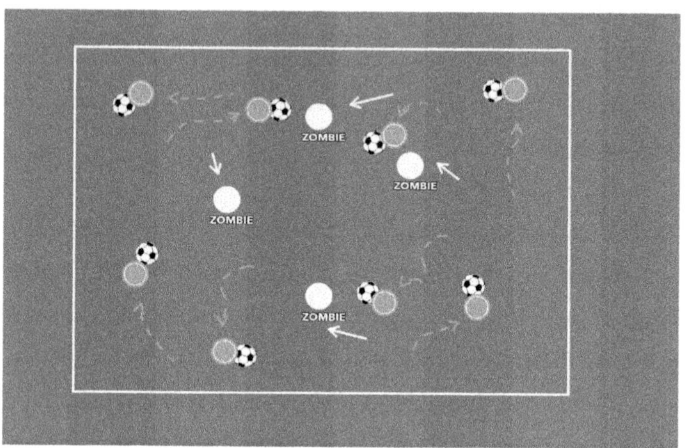
ZOMBIE
ZOMBIE
ZOMBIE
ZOMBIE

Chapter Twenty-Nine

TIP 27 - EMAIL THE PARENTS A PRACTICE SESSION

TIP 27 - EMAIL THE PARENTS A PRACTICE SESSION.

For any children that can't make training or that want to do extra at home, a short practice session is handy for the parents to have. They can refer to it and help their child practise at home. Remember, we want to have the children getting as many touches on the ball as possible at this age. This is so they become familiar and comfortable with the ball and get the basics down pat.

As I mentioned earlier, you may only have the kids for a one hour training session a week, so practise at home is even more important to get the time on the ball.

It can be a simple practise plan such as this which would only take 15-20 minutes:

AT HOME PRACTISE PLAN:

15-20 MINUTES PER DAY (OR TWICE A DAY IF POSSIBLE)

- 20 Sole Rolls each foot x 2
- 30 Toe Taps each foot x 2
- 30 Happy Feet x 2
- 20 Passes between two cones x 2
- 20 wall passes x 2
- 3 minutes of bounce juggling*
- 5 minutes of dribbling through obstacles
- 5 minutes of shooting at a target

Points to remember:

Use both feet; Do it correctly - it doesn't have to be 100 miles an hour while you are learning; Have fun! *Note: "Bounce juggling" is when the ball bounces between every touch. It is used when at the children's early development as juggling is too hard, so allowing the ball to bounce inbetween gives them more time to adjust their bodies into the correct position.

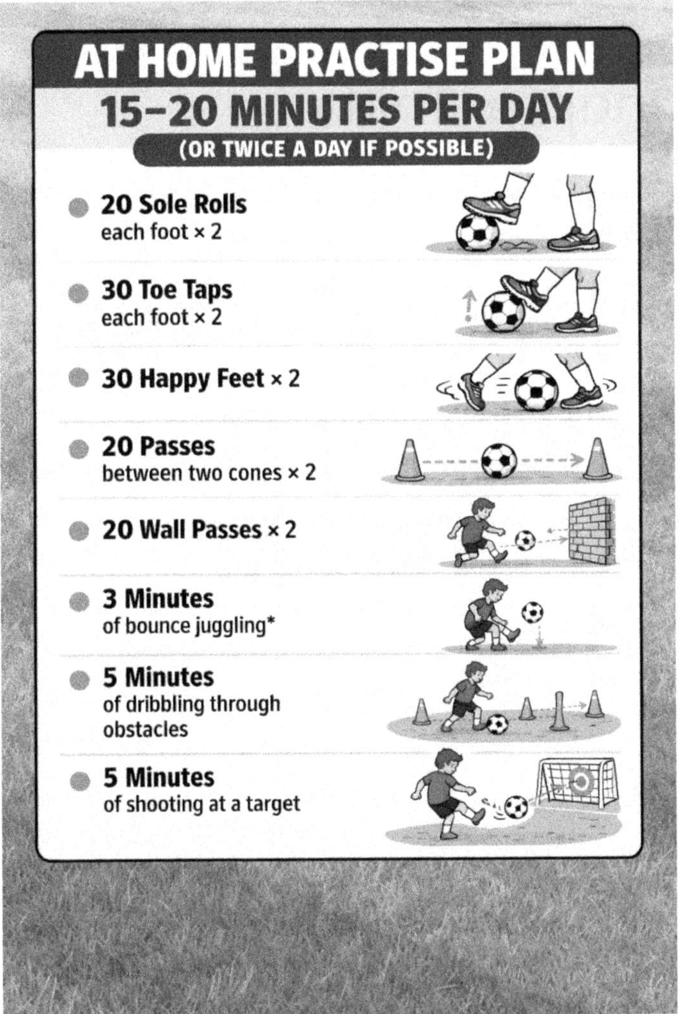
AT HOME PRACTISE PLAN
15–20 MINUTES PER DAY
(OR TWICE A DAY IF POSSIBLE)
20 Sole Rolls
each foot × 2
30 Toe Taps
each foot × 2
30 Happy Feet × 2
20 Passes
between two cones × 2
20 Wall Passes × 2
3 Minutes
of bounce juggling*
5 Minutes
of dribbling through
obstacles
5 Minutes
of shooting at a target

Chapter Thirty

TIP 28 - ENCOURAGE THE CHILDREN TO PRACTISE AT HOME

You may only have the kids for an hour during the week and then for match day. By the time next week's practice comes around, the kids may have forgotten what they learnt the previous week.

So if they can practise just 15 minutes a day, this is an extra 90 hours a year (what if they practised an extra hour a day compared to those that didn't?!). If they do this, they will improve out of sight.

So how do you get them to practise at home?

The parents can be the key here. Firstly, the child will need a soccer ball. So mention to the parents at the start of the season to buy their children a soccer ball if they haven't already. Or you could buy a whole lot of balls and give them out and ask for reimbursement from the parents. Size 3 is the correct size ball for 3 to 6 year olds.

Once they've got a ball, the parent can head out in the backyard or garage and play with them for 15 minutes anytime. I used to play with a tennis ball in the hallway at home 1v1 with my dad, which improved my skills immensely! There's really no excuse for not being able to practise.

Note: It may be worth getting a soft soccer ball for inside. That way the kids can dribble in a spare room or pass it down the hallway without damaging anything.

How do the kids know what to practise?

The basic skills and games that they learn at your training sessions are what they need to practise at home to improve. Flicks and tricks will come as they get comfortable on the ball and can try harder things. But initially, lots of touches on the ball (toe taps, moving the ball in triangles, passing off a wall, happy feet, etc.) are the key.

What if they forget how to do the skills or are doing them incorrectly?

You obviously want the children practising correct techniques. So once again, this is where the parents come in! They can show the children the correct way.

I find the best way to get interaction from the parents, and to get them to learn what the kids are learning, is to involve them in a warm-up drill or exercise at the start of training.

This way they connect with their children. Plus, they can see what the kids are learning first-hand and learn it themselves. Then they can show the kids the proper technique when they practise at home.

Blatant plug: I have an online soccer coaching course, *"How To Coach Kids Soccer – Ages 5 to 10"*, on the online learning site Udemy .com.

Udemy.com Coaching Kids Soccer Course
It's got heaps of valuable information for parents, coaches, and volunteers who want to learn the basics of how to take a children's soccer training session, what skills to teach, how to coach different types of players, how to plan a training session, plus heaps more!

Chapter Thirty-One

TIP 29 - HOW TO GET CHILDREN TO STOP AND LISTEN

TIP 29 – HOW TO GET CHILDREN TO STOP AND LISTEN

Kids are like 40-year-old men. When you're talking to them, they don't always stop what they're doing and listen!

The best way I've found to increase the chances of kids listening to you is to use one of the following three methods:

1. "Bums on ball"

Get them to sit on the ball when you are talking. Simply say, *"Bums on ball!"* and watch them quickly sit down and look at you. This stops them kicking the ball while you are speaking.

2. "Hands on heads" (or shoulders or hips)

Simply say, *"Hands on heads!"* and they will soon relate this to stopping what they are doing, putting their hands on their heads, and listening to you.

Plus, none of them wants to be last, so they all do it quickly! Give a quick high five to the first couple of players that do it (positive reinforcement).

3. Soccer pose

This is a fun one. Show the kids how to do an *"I'm the greatest soccer player going around"* pose.

Get them to:

Put one foot on top of the ball

Cross their arms across their chest

Turn their head to one side

Squint their eyes a bit

This will make them look like Eric Cantona — like they're unstoppable on the football pitch!

They'll enjoy it, and most importantly, it makes them stop what they're doing and focus on you.

Chapter Thirty-Two

TIPS 30 to 38

TIP 30 – HELPING SHY CHILDREN

If you have shy or nervous children, don't force them to do anything they don't want to do.

Get down to their height when explaining things. Smile, be calm, and use encouraging language.

If needed, hold their hand and walk through drills with them to help build their confidence.

Let them know it's normal to feel nervous:

"Everyone feels a bit nervous when they try something new, so that's okay."

Give them time, support, and small wins — their confidence will grow.

TIP 31 – LEARNING KIDS' NAMES

At the start of the season, you may not know many of the kids' names — and they won't know each other either.

A simple game to help with this:

Get the players in a circle, with you standing in the middle holding a ball.

Pass the ball to a child, and when they pass it back, they say their name.

Another option:

Set up 2 or 4 short lines.

Players pass the ball back and forth, saying their name as they pass, then go to the back of the line.

Yes, I know I said no lines, laps, or lectures... but this is a one-off! And because the lines are short, they'll still get plenty of touches.

***

PAPERBACK OR EBOOK:

Reviewed by 37 readers with a 4.5 star rating, this is my most popular book.

Start with this book:

COACHING KIDS SOCCER - AGES 5 TO 10 - Volumes 1,2,3

***

TIP 32 – NUMBER OF PLAYERS IN TRAINING GAMES

At training, when playing games, keep numbers small.

For toddlers:

- 2v2 or 3v3

For 5–6 year olds:

- 3v3 or 4v4 (5v5 at a push)

Most of the time, avoid goalkeepers. Use mini goals instead so players get more chances to score.

With smaller numbers:

- More touches on the ball

- More chances to attack and defend
- More passing opportunities
- More shots on goal

This is where the real learning happens.

TIP 33 – GOALKEEPER

Every couple of sessions, set aside time for shooting practice and let every player have a turn in goal.

Some children will be natural goalkeepers. Others may struggle with coordination or even move out of the way of the ball.

Don't expect too much at this age.

Explain that goalkeeper is an important position. Encourage them to try their best and not be afraid of the ball.

Most shots will be along the ground — not many top-corner screamers at this level!

Usually, they'll be:

- Coming out to gather the ball
- Getting a foot or hand to stop it

Give them simple, clear tips:

- Stand in the middle of the goal, about 5–6 yards out
- If the ball is on the left, move slightly left and protect that post
- If in doubt, kick it out
- Keep hands ready to catch or block

- If you catch it, hold it against your chest for control
- Throw, roll, or kick it out — whatever feels comfortable

Plant the seed early.
If they enjoy it, they'll improve naturally over time.

TIP 34 – DON'T WORRY IF YOUR TRAINING SESSION DOESN'T GO AS PLANNED!

You may need to change things or adjust on the fly during a training session — and that's completely normal.

This can happen for a number of reasons:

- A drill doesn't work as you expected (especially the first time you try it)
- The children don't understand it or it hasn't been demonstrated clearly
- A player gets injured, leaving you short on numbers
- The kids are really enjoying a drill, but you've planned to move on
- You arrive late or don't have time to set everything up properly

Never fear! Part of your job as a coach is to adapt to different situations.

If a drill isn't working, simply stop it and move on to something else.
Make a quick mental note of why it didn't work so you can adjust it next time.

On the flip side, if the kids are really enjoying a drill, let it run longer than planned!

Who cares if you have to cut another drill short?

Your main job is to make sure the kids are having fun.

Note:

It's always a good idea to have a couple of tried and tested "go-to" drills up your sleeve.

Pick two favourites and commit them to memory so you can use them anytime.

You can't go wrong with:

"Simon Says"

"Gates"

Or just playing a game

TIP 35 – WHAT SHOULD YOU/WE DO WHEN...?

It can really help to have a quick question-and-answer chat with your team every now and then — even if it's just for a couple of minutes at the start or end of training.

A great way to do this is by asking:

"What should you/we do when...?"

This can relate to football situations or general behaviour.

Here are some examples:

Q: What should we do when you get a corner?

A: The nearest player puts the ball in the corner and kicks it towards the goal.

Q: What should we do when the ball goes out on the left and it's our throw-in?

A: The left-sided player takes the throw-in and looks for a teammate.

Q: What should we do when an opposition player is being rude?

A: Smile, ignore them, or say "Have a nice day."

Q: What should we do when a teammate isn't sure what to do?

A: Help them — show or tell them what to do.

Q: What should we do if a teammate is upset?

A: Give them encouragement, support them, and if needed, get the coach.

Q: What should we do when we win, lose, or draw?

A: Shake hands with the opposition and referee, then enjoy the rest of the day.

Simple discussions like this:

- Create a positive team environment
- Teach good habits
- Help players understand expectations

Keep it short, keep it simple, and if possible, act it out using the kids to keep them engaged.

TIP 36 – SHADOW A COACH

If you are new to coaching and want to gain experience, a great way to start is to *shadow* another coach.

Ask someone at your club if there's a kids' coach you can observe for a session or two.

This allows you to see:

- How they set up drills
- How they interact with the children

- How they organise sessions
- Where equipment is kept

After shadowing for a couple of sessions, ask if you can run one of the drills.

This removes the pressure of leading a full session, and you'll still have the experienced coach there to support you if needed.

TIP 37 – ASK THE KIDS!

When teaching a skill, don't just tell the children what to do — ask them questions.

This helps them think, engage, and remember.

For example, during a passing drill, you could ask:

"Which part of the foot do we use to pass?"

Answer: The instep.

"Why do we use that part?"

Answer: Because it gives a larger surface area to strike the ball.

Try to frame your coaching points as questions:

"We try to keep our heads up when dribbling so we can see what's around us, don't we?"

"When we're dribbling, what should we try to do at the same time?"

"When we're shooting, where should we aim?"

This keeps players involved and helps them learn faster.

TIP 38 – SET SOME GOALS FOR THE COACH (YOU!)

It's important to have clear goals as a coach. Here are a few key ones to focus on:

1. Improve the children's skills

Use clear demonstrations, then let them practise through simple, fun drills.

Encourage extra practice at home where possible.

2. Encourage the children at every opportunity

Use positive language and feedback:

- Smiles
- High fives
- Thumbs up

This builds confidence and keeps them engaged.

3. Promote good sportsmanship

Children won't always win — and that's okay.

- Help them understand how to behave properly:

- Shake hands with opponents
- Don't complain when things don't go their way
- Show respect to teammates, opponents, and referees

The earlier they learn this, the better.

Chapter Thirty-Three

TIPS 39 to 45 - MATCH DAY TIPS

TIP 39 – SET INDIVIDUAL & TEAM GOALS FOR MATCH DAYS

This doesn't mean aiming to win the league or beat every team by 5 goals.

It's about setting small, achievable goals that:

- Keep players motivated
- Give them direction and purpose
- Build team spirit
- Help them develop as people

Examples of simple goals:

- Help a teammate up if they fall
- Help an opposition player up

- Pass to a teammate closer to goal
- Celebrate goals together (including the goalkeeper)
- Call for the ball (great for shy players)
- Make at least 5 tackles per half
- Take a player on 1v1

Goals outside of matches:

- Practise for 15 minutes at home (dribbling, passing, shooting)
- Learn a new skill from YouTube
- Do 3 juggles in a row
- Nutmeg the family pet!
- Learn where their favourite player grew up

TIP 40 – KIDS DON'T LIKE TO PASS THE BALL

At this age, kids often don't understand passing properly.

Their thinking is usually:

"If I pass it, I might not get it back."

So don't worry if:

- They dribble a lot
- They don't pass much
- Passes are misplaced

Just keep encouraging passing — it will come naturally over time as they develop.

Important:

Try not to let parents shout "Pass the ball!" constantly from the sidelines.

Players will learn to pass as their individual skills improve.

TIP 41 – TRY PLAYERS IN DIFFERENT POSITIONS

At this age, it's important that players experience all positions.

They should:

- Defend
- Attack
- Play in midfield
- Be in 1v1 situations
- Try being a goalkeeper

This helps them:

- Understand the game better
- Develop all-round skills
- Find what they enjoy most

Over time, they may prefer certain positions — but early on, mix it up.

TIP 42 – DECISION MAKING

As a coach, don't make every decision for the players.

If you constantly tell them:

- Where to be
- When to pass
- When to shoot

They won't learn to think for themselves.

During training:

- You can pause play
- Show better options
- Guide their thinking

During matches:

- Let them play
- Let them make mistakes
- Let them learn

Also, they won't take in much from the sidelines anyway!

If you need to coach something:

- Do it at half-time
- Or when they're off the pitch

TIP 43 – FIND A HELPER

You don't have to do everything yourself.

Having help can make a big difference:

- Managing equipment

- Organising players
- Stepping in if you're away or ill

If you have a large group, it's especially useful.
Ask:

- A parent
- Another volunteer
- An older player (U16/U18)

Most people are happy to help if you ask.

TIP 44 – DON'T CRITICISE OTHERS

Never criticise:

- The opposition
- Other coaches
- Parents
- Referees

This sets a bad example for your players.
If they see you:

- Complaining
- Arguing
- Being negative

They'll think it's okay to do the same.

Especially referees:

- They're giving up their time
- They will make mistakes (like everyone)

Respect them and thank them.

Set the standard for how your team behaves.

Note:

Remind parents that the game is for the kids — not for shouting instructions from the sidelines.

TIP 45 – KEEP POSITIONS SIMPLE

Keep things simple on match day.

At this age:

- Players won't stick to positions for long
- They'll naturally follow the ball

If you're playing 5-a-side (1 goalkeeper + 4 outfield):

Set up:

- 2 defenders
- 2 attackers

Tell each player where to start:

"You start on the left in defence"

"You start on the right in attack"

This helps them know where to begin each half or restart.

For throw-ins / kick-ins:

- Left side = left player takes it
- Right side = right player takes it

If that doesn't work:

- Let the nearest player take it

Simple messages:

To defenders:

"Your job is to stop the other team shooting."

To attackers:

"Have fun, take players on, and try to score."

Keep it basic, link it back to training, and let them play.

Chapter Thirty-Four

8 KIDS SOCCER GAMES

8 KIDS SOCCER GAMES

Here are some simple kids' soccer games to get you started on your coaching journey.

All are easy to set up and focus on the key fundamentals:

- Dribbling
- Passing
- Shooting
- 1v1

If you'd like more games with detailed descriptions, diagrams, progressions, and coach notes, head over to:

www.chriskingsoccercoach.com
or search **"Chris King Soccer"**.

Note:

Kids develop at different rates. Some will pick things up quickly, others will take more time.

Always create an environment where every child can experience success.

In some of the games below, players are asked to beat their *own* score (personal best).

This means they are improving against themselves — not comparing to others.

GAME 1 – GATES

Set up 5–6 pairs of cones (about 2 yards apart) around a square. These are the "gates".

Players must dribble through as many gates as possible in 1 minute.

After the first round:

Ask how many gates they got through

Go again and try to beat their score

Focus:

- Dribbling
- Close control
- Changing direction

Coaching tip:

If players can't stop the ball quickly when you say "Stop", they are likely kicking and chasing instead of using small touches.

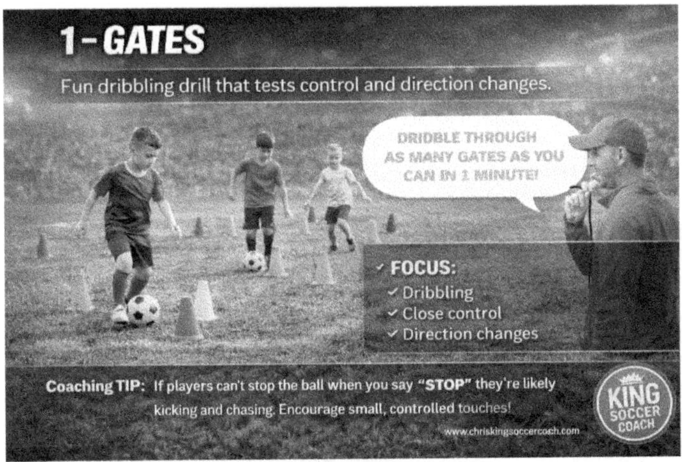

FUN KIDS SOCCER GAME: GATES

GAME 2 – TAG

All players have a ball and dribble inside an area.

1–2 players are "taggers" (no ball).

When a tagger touches a player:

That player leaves their ball

They become a tagger

Last player remaining wins.

Focus:

- Dribbling
- Changing direction
- Awareness (scanning for taggers)

Note:

Taggers are essentially defenders — they're learning how to:

Read movement

Close players down

Block space

FUN KIDS SOCCER GAME: TAG

GAME 3 – OUCH!

Players dribble around and try to kick their ball at the coach (below the knee).

When hit, the coach reacts with:

"OUCH!" or something silly/funny

Play for 1 minute:

How many times can each player hit the coach?

Focus:

- Shooting

- Dribbling
- Striking a moving ball

FUN KIDS SOCCER GAME: OUCH

GAME 4 – I CAN DO THIS, CAN YOU?

All players (and the coach) have a ball in a large area.

Players take turns saying:

"I can do this, can you?"

Then they perform something:

- A trick
- A turn
- A fake

- A speed move
- Something silly (e.g. acting like a chicken!)

The coach calls the next player.

Focus:

- Creativity
- Confidence
- Fun

Coaching tip:

Great as a warm-up or when you have a spare 5–10 minutes.

FUN KIDS SOCCER GAME: I CAN DO THIS, CAN YOU?

GAME 5 – GRAB THE CONE

Spread cones randomly around the area.

Players must:

- Dribble out
- Pick up a cone
- Dribble back and give it to the coach (or stack it)

Play for 1 minute:

- How many cones can they collect?
- Try to beat their score next round

Focus:

Close control

Head up (awareness)

Progression:

Pair players up

Assign cone colours to each pair

First team to collect all their cones wins

Tip:

If you don't have cones, use anything — shoes, bottles, etc.

FUN KIDS SOCCER GAME: GRAB THE CONE

GAME 6 – DODGEM CARS

Each player has:

- A ball
- A cone (held like a steering wheel)
- Players dribble around and "beep" when near others.

Coach calls instructions:

- Turn left / right
- Speed up
- Reverse
- Red light / green light

Focus:

- Dribbling

- Awareness
- Listening skills

FUN KIDS SOCCER GAME: DODGEM CARS

GAME 7 – DEFEND THE CONE

Set up:

- Small square or circle
- 1 cone in the middle
- 3 attackers around the outside, 1 defender in the middle

Attackers:

- Pass the ball
- Try to hit the cone

Defender:

Tries to block passes/shots

After 1 minute:

Swap defender

Challenge:

Who can defend the cone best?

Focus:

- Defending
- Passing
- Shooting

GAME 8 – 2v2 / 3v3 GAME

Set up small pitches and play:

2v2 or 3v3

Rotate teams every few minutes.

Use:

Mini goals

Or cones as goals

Focus:

- Dribbling
- Passing
- Shooting
- 1v1 situations

This is where everything comes together.

FUN KIDS SOCCER GAME: 2V2'S, 3V3'S

Chapter Thirty-Five

"4 GOAL FUN SOCCER"

FOCUS OF SESSION:

Let the kids learn by playing - just play soccer and have fun like they would at lunchtime at school. All skills will be worked on naturally.

SET UP:

- **6 to 12 players**
- 35x25 yard rectangle
- 4 mini goals

THE DRILL:

We want the kids to learn by doing, have success (i.e. score goals!) and not worry about any consequences of making mistakes. So let them play soccer and score lots of goals!

Set up a 35x25 yard rectangle with 4 goals (one on each side).

Split the players into 4 teams (ie if 8 players have 4 teams of 2. If you only have 6 players, have 3 teams of 2).

All teams play at once and can score in any goal!

As soon as a ball goes out or a goal is scored the coach should put another one in straight away. Also, sometimes put two balls at once! Twice the chaos, twice the fun and twice the goals.

The first team to 5 goals wins, then swap teams around.

COACHES NOTES:

- Make sure everyone is having fun! Lots of encouragement and celebrating when goals are scored (high fives, rolly pollies, etc!).

- Encourage players to dribble, pass, take players on and shoot. This is a great chance for them to work out how to do things in a game situation.

CHANGE IT:

#1 - Combine two teams (ie 4v4.). No need to even stop the game, just call out "Blues and greens are together versus yellow and reds."

#2 - Play 3 teams v 1. And if it's too hard for the 1 team, maybe the coach can join in and help them?

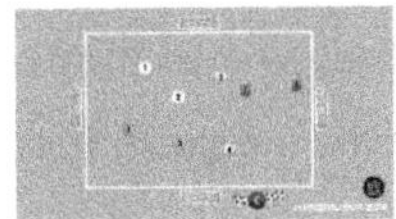

4 teams with 2 players each - players can score in any goal. This drill is all about having fun and scoring goals. Players get to practise all the skills they are learning (dribbling, passing, taking players on and shooting) in a fun environment.

Chapter Thirty-Six

FINAL THOUGHTS – KEEP IT SIMPLE, KEEP IT FUN

FINAL THOUGHTS – KEEP IT SIMPLE, KEEP IT FUN

Coaching young children (ages 3 to 6) isn't about tactics, formations, or winning games. It's about giving them a **great first experience of football**.

If they leave your sessions smiling, excited, and wanting to come back next week — you've done your job.

Focus on the Basics

At this age, stick to the core skills:

- Dribbling
- Passing

- Shooting
- 1v1 situations

You don't need anything complicated. Simple games that keep kids active and involved are always best. Create a Positive Environment

Children learn best when they feel:

- Safe
- Encouraged
- Free to make mistakes

Celebrate effort more than results. A big cheer for trying something new goes a long way.

Keep Sessions Moving

Avoid long explanations. Show them quickly, then let them play.

The more touches they get on the ball, the more they improve.

Be Patient

Every child develops at a different pace. Some will pick things up quickly, others will take time.

That's completely normal. Your role is to support them all and make sure everyone feels included.

Enjoy It Yourself

If you're enjoying the session, the kids will too.

Bring energy, be positive, and don't be afraid to join in the fun.

YOUR IMPACT AS A COACH

You might not realise it, but you're doing something important.

You're helping children:

-Build confidence

-Learn teamwork

-Stay active

-Develop a love for the game

For many of them, this is their **first experience of football** — and you shape how they see it.

FINAL TIP

-Keep it simple.

-Keep it active.

-Keep it fun.

Do that, and you'll be a great coach.

Keep on coaching!

Chris King

View my most popular kids coaching book and online course here:

PAPERBACK OR EBOOK:

Reviewed by 37 readers with a 4.5 star rating, this is my most popular book.

Start with this book:

COACHING KIDS SOCCER - AGES 5 TO 10 - Volumes 1,2,3:

ONLINE COACHING COURSE:

Taken by 479 students with a 4.5 star rating, this is my most popular course.

Start with this course:

HOW TO COACH KIDS SOCCER / FOOTBALL (BEGINNER COURSE)

A simple introduction to:

- Coaching young players
- Planning sessions
- Understanding the basics of grassroots football
- Ideal for parents and volunteers just starting out.

www.ingramcontent.com/pod-product-compliance
Ingram Content Group UK Ltd.
Pitfield, Milton Keynes, MK11 3LW, UK
UKHW021648190726
13853UKWH00001B/138